Origins

The Trojan Horse

Tony Bradman ✳ Jonatronix

OXFORD
UNIVERSITY PRESS

Chapter 1 – An invitation

Max, Cat, Ant and Tiger were heading to the micro-den in the park. Cat, Ant and Tiger were talking excitedly about their plans for the afternoon.

"What's wrong, Max?" asked Cat, noticing Max was unusually quiet.

"I'm thinking about Dr X," he said. "Do you realize we haven't seen any X-bots for almost a *month*? Don't you think that's strange?"

"Isn't that a good thing?" replied Cat.

"I suppose so," said Max. "It's just … it's odd."

"Relax, Max," laughed Tiger. "You worry too much. Maybe he's *finally* given up."

"Tiger's right," said Cat. "We should forget about him and enjoy ourselves."

"I don't trust him," said Max, as much to himself as to the others. He sighed. He just couldn't shake the feeling that Dr X was up to something.

Meanwhile …

Dr X reclined in his chair. He propped his feet on his desk – it was piled high with books. A broad smile stretched across his face.

Plug and Socket knocked on the door. "Er, are you OK, Boss?" asked Plug nervously through the door. Dr X had been behaving oddly for a few days now. All they'd heard from him was the occasional wicked chuckle.

"Yes, fine, fine. Everything's fine," answered Dr X.

Plug and Socket looked at each other. "Do you think he's *really* all right?" said Plug. "Should we break down the door to check?"

Before Socket could answer, the door slid open and Dr X emerged from his lair, clutching a book. Plug and Socket jumped back, looking guilty.

"Come on, you two. We've got work to do," Dr X said, unusually cheerful.

"Yes Boss, sorry Boss," said Socket. "What's the job?"

"All will be revealed," smiled Dr X. "Let's just say it's *amazing* what you can learn from a good book."

With that, he hurried off, whistling.

Plug and Socket looked at each other, even more confused than usual.

Chapter 2 – X-traordinary games

"Look, all I'm saying is that I think we need to stay here and make sure our defences are as strong as possible," said Max, looking around the micro-den.

"Come on, Max," said Ant. "This is too good a chance to miss. *Everyone* in Greenville has got an invitation – if we don't leave soon, we might not get in."

It was true. Everyone had been invited to the grand opening of X-traordinary Games. However, no one had seen who had delivered the invitations. Max had run downstairs when he heard the doorbell. He'd pulled open the front door but no one was there. All he saw was a small purple van driving away.

You are invited this Saturday
to the grand opening
of Greenville's newest
computer games store –

X-TRAORDINARY GAMES!

Come and try out all
the new technology,
including virtual reality
games, for free!

"Well, I'm not missing out, Max," said Tiger, heading out of the door.

Cat and Ant looked at Max.

"Come on, Max. It'll be fun," Cat said gently.

Max sighed. He really did want to go … but the strange feeling that something was going to happen just wouldn't go away.

"You could always join us later if you want!" called Cat, as they left micro-den and Max behind.

It was almost impossible to miss X-traordinary Games. A queue was already snaking down the street and excited chatter filled the air.

"It's really busy! Good job we got here early," said Cat.

As they joined the back of the queue, a girl in a purple t-shirt with a horse logo on the front came over to them.

"Hi, I'm Jo. I've been waiting for you," she said. "I've got a game I know you're going to love!" She smiled enthusiastically at them.

"I can't wait," said Tiger, as the three of them followed the girl inside. Cat couldn't help but notice the envious looks from the children waiting as they were escorted to the front of the queue and straight into the shop.

Inside, the shop was packed with children. Big screens showing computer games covered the walls, filling the room with music and the flicker of computer graphics.

Jo directed Cat, Ant and Tiger to an area tucked away in the far corner of the shop.

"These are for you," Jo said, pointing to four headsets and tablets. "But, hang on, there are only three of you, where's the fourth?"

"Max didn't want to come," replied Tiger quickly, eager to get on with the game.

"He might join us later," said Cat, feeling a little guilty about leaving Max.

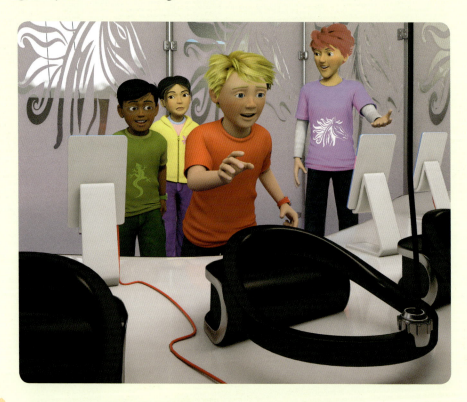

"OK. I suppose three is better than none," she sighed. "The game is all set up for you. Just pop your headsets on and record your feedback on the tablets. I'm *sure* you're going to find it extraordinary."

Cat, Ant and Tiger put on their headsets and they snapped firmly in place. Almost a little too securely but the friends were too excited to notice.

Cat beamed. "This is going to be great," she said as the screen flickered into life and the game began.

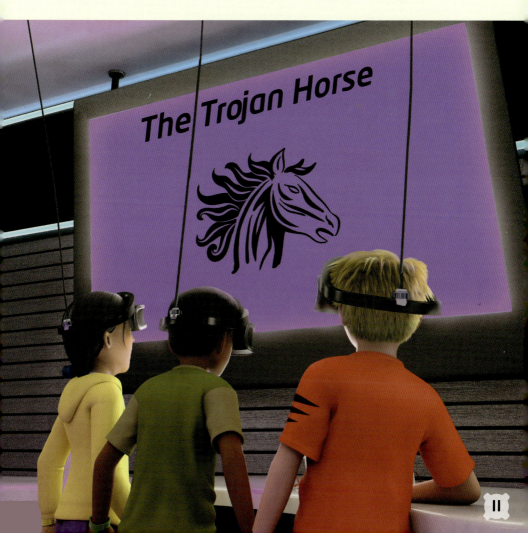

The Trojan Horse

Chapter 3 – A new world

Back at the micro-den, Max had checked everything (at least three times!) and even set up a new alarm system. He smiled to himself.

"Duty done, time for some fun!" he said, feeling better now the den was safe. He knew his friends were right – he probably *was* being overly-cautious – but at least now they were prepared if anything *did* happen.

Max set off toward the town centre, looking forward to joining his friends and trying out the new games.

When Max arrived at X-traordinary Games, the queue had disappeared but the shop was full of children. He looked around, trying to find his friends.

At last he saw them. They were at the rear of the shop, in a special area that was almost hidden from view. The three of them were gazing intently at a large screen on the wall and each was wearing a headset connected by cables to the ceiling. Max had to admit it did look great!

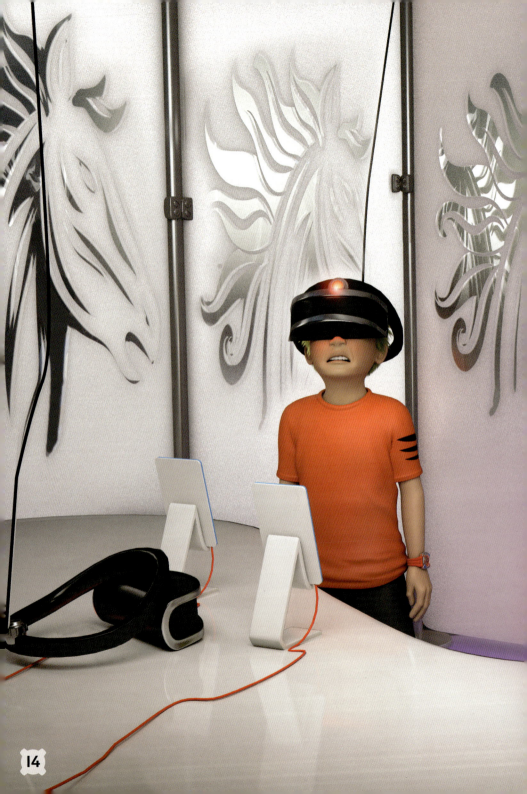

Max picked up the fourth headset, keen to join his friends in the game. As he did so, he noticed something. The other children in the shop had been moving, their hands and feet twitching as they played the games in their heads, but Cat, Ant and Tiger were as still as statues. Also, the other children's headsets weren't attached to the ceiling and they had green lights on top, not red lights like his friends.

Max looked at the game more closely – The Trojan Horse. It must be a prototype he thought as he'd not heard of it before. He had, however, read a lot of books about the Trojan War and something was bothering him. Something about the characters didn't seem quite right.

Peering closely at the screen, Max felt the hairs on the back of his neck prickle. It couldn't be! There were Xs in the game! The closer Max looked, the more he saw – on the armour, on the shields and on the walls! It could only mean one thing – Dr X was behind this.

The red lights on the headsets began to flicker. Max reached out to pull them off his friends' heads – then froze. If Dr X *was* controlling Cat, Ant and Tiger, then breaking the link might hurt them – he couldn't take that risk. He had to do something, though. He would have to join them in the virtual world.

Max reached for the spare headset on the table beneath the screen – then stopped. *If I wear the same headsets as Cat, Ant and Tiger, I'll be trapped in the game too,* he thought. *I'll have to use one of the other headsets with a green light and hope it lets me access the game.*

Max put the headset on – and gulped. He wondered if this was a good idea after all …

In the blink of an eye, Max was in the game, just outside the walls of the ancient city of Troy. He could almost feel the warm sun on his skin. It felt so real and looked exactly like the pictures in his book on Greek myths. The city was ringed by high walls guarded by warriors with plumed helmets, swords and shields.

They must be Trojan soldiers, thought Max.

Max looked down at himself. He was wearing a tunic and sandals. He was a little disappointed that he wasn't dressed in the impressive armour of the warriors.

"Keep moving!" a loud voice cried, interrupting Max's thoughts. Max darted quickly behind a nearby rock. He peered out … Cat, Ant and Tiger, dressed in Trojan tunics, were being led away by two Greek warriors.

They were marching in step, like robots. Their faces were totally blank.

"I hope we've got the right ones," said the tall warrior. "In these tunics they all look the same."

"I hope so," said the short one. "We don't want to get in trouble with the Boss again!"

Max could see that the two soldiers were deep in conversation but he was too far away to hear what they were saying. Something about them looked familiar but before he could get a look at their faces, they moved on towards the seashore.

In the distance, Max could see ship after ship bobbing on the water. All along the shoreline, hundreds of tents fluttered in the breeze – it was the Greek army's camp. Max watched as his three friends were led into a large, important-looking tent. He hurried after them.

Chapter 4 – A close escape

Max crept through the Greek camp and slipped into the large tent, ducking down behind a wooden chest near the entrance. Inside, the tent was like a room in a great palace. He had to admit Dr X had done a good job creating this world.

"Welcome, welcome!" boomed a voice from the back of the tent. Max watched as his friends were ushered towards an ornate throne. There, in all his finery, sat Agamemnon, the Greek king.

Cat, Ant and Tiger were lined up in front of the king and the two warriors stood behind, guarding them. Around the perimeter of the tent, an army of X-bots stood watching. It was going to be tough getting out of here.

"Ah, I love it when a plan comes together," said the king, rubbing his hands in delight. "Plug. Socket. I make a good King Agamemnon, don't I?"

Max *knew* it! He thought that voice sounded familiar! He peered over the chest to see Dr X beaming beneath the shadow of his golden helmet.

"King Aga what? Does that mean you're not Dr X any more?" asked Socket.

"Give me strength …" muttered Dr X. "It's simple. Kids love computers so I knew those four wouldn't be able to resist an invitation to a new computer game shop. Now they're inside my world, I have them exactly where I want them and I can finally get my watches back. The rest is history, as they say," he chuckled.

Plug and Socket looked at each other, confused. "We haven't travelled back in time, have we?"

"No, the *idea* is right out of the history books. You know, the Trojan Horse? For goodness sake! The Greeks tricked the Trojans by giving them a gift of a large wooden horse. What the Trojans didn't know was that inside the horse were Greek soldiers. Once the horse was wheeled into the city of Troy, the Greeks jumped out and took over the city!"

Plug and Socket looked at each other blankly.

"Must I explain *everything?*" said Dr X. "Like the Trojans, I too have played a trick. The computer game is my Trojan Horse! Anyway, on to more important things. Where is Number Four?"

Plug and Socket scratched their helmeted heads.

"The fourth child," repeated Dr X his voice growing louder.

"I knew we'd end up in trouble," muttered Plug.

"I need all *four*, you buffoons!" hollered Dr X. "Go and find the other one. He must be somewhere nearby. They are *always* together."

Max watched as Plug and Socket turned and shuffled towards him. He hid further behind the chest, hoping he hadn't been seen.

"Now, where are my manners?" Dr X said, his stare fixed on Cat, Ant and Tiger.

"You must be tired. Here, come and sit down – but first, make yourselves comfortable. Take off those heavy … bracelets, yes that's it … those heavy bracelets. They must be weighing you down."

Max's heart sank as he poked his head over the chest just in time to see Cat, Ant and Tiger taking their bracelets off. Max froze. *If they've taken their bracelets off in the game does that mean they've taken their watches off in real life?* he thought. He had to get out of the game and find out.

As Max slowly backed away, he lost his balance. (He wasn't used to wearing sandals!) He grabbed the wall and with a loud rip the side of the tent split open.

"There he is!" roared Dr X. "Grab him!"

The X-bot soldiers raced towards him but Max ducked down and shot out of the tent. He ran across the sandy plain with the X-bots in hot pursuit.

In no time at all, half a dozen more X-bots appeared out of thin air. They circled in front of Max and he skidded to a stop. He was surrounded.

The X-bots surged forward but Max swerved round them and ran towards Troy. The X-bot soldiers followed – they weren't far behind.

Then Max stopped. *I'm inside a game,* he remembered. He almost laughed. His mind wasn't being controlled by Dr X so he could remove his headset whenever he wanted to. He raised his hands to the golden wreath wrapped around his head. Nothing happened. He tugged again and this time a strange feeling swept over him – as if he were in two places at once. Then slowly, the game started to fade around him.

Chapter 5 – Rescue!

Max blinked as the shop slowly came back into focus. Everything around him looked the same as before but he knew he didn't have much time. Dr X wouldn't stop until he had all four watches.

The watches, Max thought. *They must be here somewhere.* He looked around him.

"Can I help you?" said Jo, coming over. "Do you need a hand getting started?"

"No, I'm OK, thanks," answered Max quickly. He needed to find the watches.

"Are you with these three?" Jo asked, gesturing towards Cat, Ant and Tiger.

"Er, no," answered Max. "I was just looking at this game. What is it by the way?"

"It's our latest release – The Trojan Horse. It's … look, you shouldn't be in here," said Jo, her mood suddenly changing. "This is a reserved area." She gestured for him to follow her.

As soon as Jo's back was turned, Max sneaked back to his friends.

He walked towards the motionless Cat, Ant and Tiger. "The watches have to be …" he started. There they were. Just sitting in a box on the table. Dr X was obviously going to send someone to pick them up later. Well, not if Max had anything to do with it.

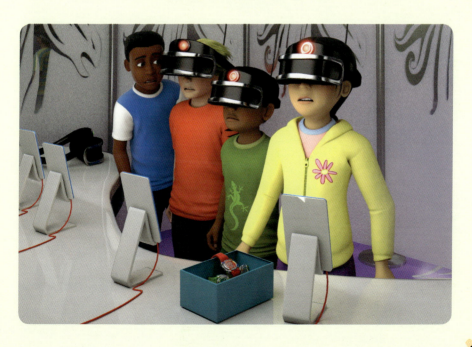

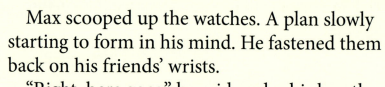

Max scooped up the watches. A plan slowly starting to form in his mind. He fastened them back on his friends' wrists.

"Right, here goes," he said under his breath, hoping his friends wouldn't be hurt by what he was about to do.

One by one, he turned the dial on each of their watches and pressed the X. They shrank instantly, their headsets left dangling in mid-air.

"*You* again!" came a voice from behind Max. "What are you doing back in here? Where have the other three gone?"

Max could feel his heart pounding in his chest. He hoped his plan had worked.

"It looks like they've gone. I thought it'd be OK for me to play now the game's free …" he answered, trying to sound confident.

"Gone? Where to?" Jo turned around as if searching for them. "Oh, no! This is not good – not good at all. Let me know if you see them, will you? Two boys and a girl." The assistant stormed off.

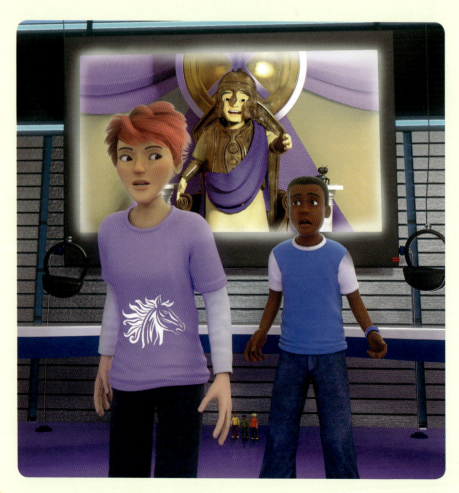

Max desperately looked around the room. What if breaking the link to the game had really hurt his friends?

"Hey, you made it!" came a voice from behind Max.

Max whirled around to see Cat, Ant and Tiger smiling at him, now normal size.

"You missed a really strange game," said Ant, rubbing his head.

"Yeah," said Tiger. "I haven't got a clue what happened – we were in this strange tent and …"

Max patted Tiger on the shoulder. "Let *me* tell it – it really is an amazing story!"

Chapter 6 – The Trojans fight back

Cat, Ant and Tiger were stunned. They couldn't believe how close they'd come to losing their watches.

"But it felt so real," murmured Cat.

"I know," said Max, "Dr X did a good job creating the game. His plan might just have worked if …"

"If you'd come with us instead of staying at the den," finished Tiger, looking a bit sheepish.

The four children looked at each other. Max didn't like to say it but Tiger had a point – Max had been right to be suspicious. It had been a very close escape.

"We should get out of here," said Ant. "We don't know what else Dr X has up his tunic sleeve!"

"I have another idea," said Max, smiling. "Dr X is not the only one who knows his Greek myths. How about we help King Agamemnon relive history?"

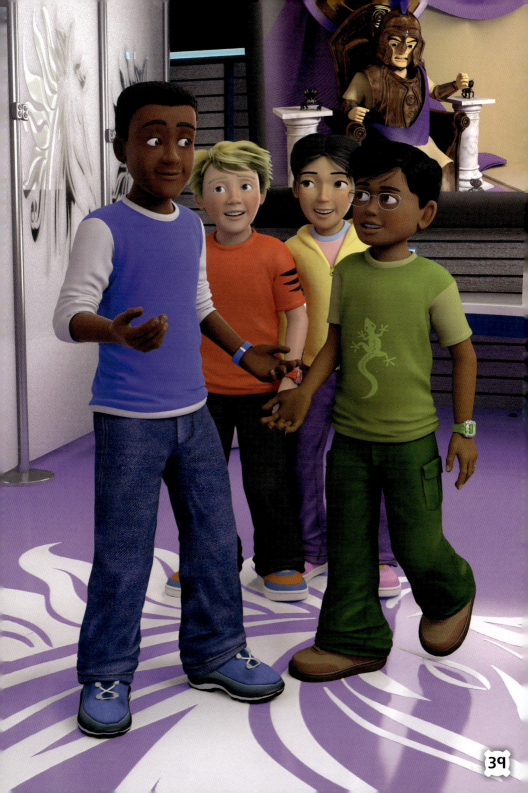

"What do you have in mind?" asked Cat.

"Well, the Trojan War had many battles – I think it's time for another one, don't you?"

"There are only four of us, though," said Ant. "That's hardly an army."

"We could ask the others to help," suggested Cat, looking round the room.

"Great idea!" said Tiger, excited at the idea of battling Dr X.

"How will we access the game without Dr X controlling us, though?" asked Ant.

"I used one of the other headsets last time and it worked. Dr X, I mean King Agamemnon, won't know what's hit him!"

Chapter 7 – Finale!

Back in the game, Dr X wasn't happy. "Where did they go?" he roared. "They can't just disappear!"

"I don't know, Boss," said Plug, gasping for breath. "We looked everywhere. Socket's still …"

"You two are useless. Totally useless. I'd be better off doing everything myself. All you had to do was catch the fourth one. He was right under our …"

"You'd better come quick, Boss," said Socket, running into the tent.

"Have you found him? Excellent!" cried Dr X.

"Er … not exactly," replied Socket. "We're under attack!"

"What are you talking about?" said Dr X, leaping off of his throne.

He whipped open the door of the tent. Socket was right. An army of children dressed as Trojan soldiers was charging towards the tent. "Oh no," he moaned. "Those pesky kids …"

The hoard of children surged towards the tent. They were enjoying themselves – it was far more realistic than the other games! Plug and Socket ran out of the tent and Dr X limped behind, struggling to escape in his heavy armour.

Back at the shop, the children groaned as the screens fizzed and went black. So many children had joined in the game, the computers had overloaded – Dr X's virtual world was no more.

By the end of the day, the shop had closed, never to open again.

As the last of the children headed home, Max, Cat, Ant and Tiger returned to their den. They knew that it wasn't the last they'd heard of Dr X but for now it felt good. They had outwitted the great King Agamemnon and defeated the Trojan Horse. It had been close but the next time they would be ready.

Meanwhile …

"Do you think he's OK in there?" whispered Plug, his ear pressed against the door to Dr X's lair.

"He seemed pretty angry and he said his feet were hurting after running all that way in sandals … even if it was only 'virtual' running!" answered Socket.

"Yeah, and he wasn't too happy when he lost the remote control and couldn't stop the game," said Plug. "Lucky for him those children broke it!"

The pair looked at each other and chuckled. Well, it was pretty funny …

A note from the author

I've always been fascinated by the story of the Trojan War. The Greeks had been besieging Troy for 10 years and didn't think they would ever conquer it. Then they came up with the idea of tricking the Trojans – they pretended to sail away but left a giant wooden horse outside the walls of the city. The Trojans thought it was some kind of offering and brought it inside the walls, not knowing that lots of Greek soldiers were hiding inside it! That night they crept out – and Troy was at their mercy. I thought it would be great if this story gave Dr X an idea for a way to get the watches back – he has been 'besieging' them for a long time, after all! So a 'Trojan Horse' of his own might be just the thing …

Tony Bradman

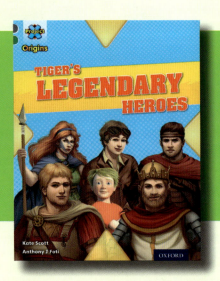

Interested in finding out more about myths and legends? Read *Tiger's Legendary Heroes*.